THE PRAYER THAT HEALS

D0589939

THE PRAYER THAT HEALS

Praying for Healing in the Family

Francis MacNutt

HODDER AND STOUGHTON
LONDON   SYDNEY   AUCKLAND

British Library Cataloguing in Publication Data
A record for this book is available from the British Library

ISBN 0 340 28079 4

Printed and bound in Great Britain by
Cox & Wyman Ltd, Reading, Berkshire

Hodder and Stoughton
A division of Hodder Headline PLC
338 Euston Road
London NW1 3BH

Contents

Introduction

Some 14 years ago I first discovered, in a
personal way, the amazing good news that
Jesus ordinarily heals people when we pray
with them — that he would even heal people
through my simple prayers. In the years that
followed I learned more about how to pray
for the sick; I encouraged others to pray and
saw them make the same glad discovery of
how good God is! Nearly every day my
friends and I saw remarkable healings take
place. The most rewarding sight of all was to
see such things as the tears of happiness
glistening on the face of an elderly woman,

free of pain for the first time in years, as she realized how much Jesus cared for her personally.

The darker side to this happy discovery of God's healing power was my growing wonderment at how Christians had come, in large measure, to lose this precious heritage of healing prayer. Some churches even question whether God heals today through anything other than natural means, like medicine. Somehow an "enemy had sown weeds in the wheat," and, as a result, many Christians simply had not learned how to pray with each other at home—for anything, much less for healing. Even Christians who come to church every Sunday have never learned to pray with each other at home. When I first began to realize this sad situation, about 1976, I started checking out my impressions by asking groups of Christians at conferences and retreats: "How many of you can remember your own father ever praying *with* you *in his own words?*" By now I have asked this simple question of more than a hundred thousand people, and their response seems to

show that only about 3% of Christians can
remember their father ever praying with
them.¹ Now, this is astonishing if it means
that about 97% of churchgoing Christians,
who presumably come from better Christian
homes than those who are not bothering to
come to retreats, have never had the experience of their father praying with them in
his own words. When I ask the same question
about mothers, the record is better, and the
percentage rises to about 20%. But still, isn't
it tragic when four out of every five cannot
remember their mother ever praying with
them in her own words?

Again, when you ask married couples if
they pray with one another, you find that the

---

1. This percentage is *remarkably* consistent in all parts of the
United States; the hands raised are seldom over 5%. The
only exception was among the students at Oral Roberts
University where about 50% could remember their fathers
praying with them. On the other hand, at one retreat for 100
seminarians not a single one could remember his father ever
praying with him. (Small wonder, then, that after ordination
they may have difficulty feeling comfortable with spontaneous
prayer meetings.) I have asked the same question in various
other countries with much the same results. At one gathering
of 2000 people in Korea only one hand went up.

vast majority—if they pray at all—only pray formal prayers, like grace at meals.

This lack of shared family prayer is a terrible personal loss, and it's so common that married couples don't even realize they are missing anything. You seldom hear a sermon about praying together; yet, it seems to me, missing out on shared prayer is a loss similar to not attending church on Sunday. For instance, many Christians feel distant from God, unsure of whether he loves them. Often this distance goes back to our childhood: If my father didn't feel close enough to God to speak to him in my presence, chances are my own religion will be very private. Probably I will resent it when I am asked to change from a quiet Sunday liturgy, where everyone leaves me alone, to one where I am supposed to sing enthusiastically or to give the people around me the kiss of peace. My relationship to God is likely to be very formal and I may find it hard to experience the kind of friendship with Jesus that he himself holds out to me: "I shall not call you servants any more. . . . I call you friends" (Jn 15:15).

If I were a young person thinking about marrying, I would make it a priority to find a partner I could pray with every day. Just today I was talking with a friend who said that he can tell a real difference on those days he does not start off praying with his wife. The metaphor he used was: "It's like walking outside without your clothes on." Without praying together it is hard to forgive each other when quarrels and misunderstandings arise. When we do pray together we have a real sense of the presence of God; something deep within us comes together.

Again, if I am living in community or with a roommate in college, what a help it is if we can pray together from time to time very simply. Many priests, brothers and sisters, whose hearts cry out for a more personal form of prayer life, suffer precisely because other members of their communities want nothing more than formal prayers.

At any rate, praying together at home is such a beautiful experience—and so easy to learn—that the present bleak record could easily be changed if people were taught and "given permission" to try. Twenty years from now, I hope, most Christian families will be experiencing the joy of praying together. So far as I know, there is no teaching in any Christian church against praying together at home; in fact, quite the contrary. This makes the poor record of actual practice all the more mysterious, unless it comes from the very human problem of priests and ministers concentrating so much on what happens in the church in formal worship that they neglect teaching families what they can do at home.

Because much of my work has been showing ordinary Christians that God will work extraordinary healings through them, I have long desired to have available a short, simple book that I could give to the people who come to me asking for prayer—a book that would show them how to pray for healing for one another when they return home.[2]

Over the years many married couples

2. Barbara Shlemon's *Healing Prayer* (Ave Maria Press) and Agnes Sanford's *Healing Light* (Logos International) are two fine books I have handed out to many friends who wanted a sound, simple book on how to pray for the sick.

have come to ask for prayer. For instance, a husband might bring his wife who was suffering from cancerous lumps. As our team would wait to pray for the wife, the husband would usually wander off to a corner of the room as if he did not consider himself expert enough to pray for his own wife. Then we would have to encourage him to join us. For the most part, husbands and wives have not prayed with their sick partner or child even in the privacy of their home. Who knows how much cancer, arthritis and heart disease could be healed if only ordinary Christians learned how to pray with one another? Again and again we have had to bring husbands and wives out of the corner, as it were, lead them to their partner and say: "You can do it. Jesus wants to use you to bless and even to heal your partner." So many Christians have never learned to pray with simple confidence and love for one another.

I hope this little book meets the need of families who want to learn, as simply as possible, how to pray at home for their needs — healing in particular.

This book is meant to show you, as simply as possible, how you can pray with your husband, your wife, your child, or your friend, for healing.

Francis S. MacNutt
May 9, 1980
Largo, Florida

One

God Still Heals Today

What God would like to do for and through you is so wonderful that you may find it hard to believe! God wants ordinary people like you to bless and heal each other in your families. When you start to pray with others, amazing things will happen to you and to your loved ones. I want to encourage you to believe a truth that Christians today are often too cynical to believe: Jesus will heal his people through *your* prayers.

If you need encouragement to pray for your sick friends, just take the example of Jesus himself. In the Gospels you see him spending a large part of his time going from one sick person to another, laying his hands on them and healing them. His heart goes out to people — like the time he was tired and tried to get away from the crowd to rest with his disciples.

> But the crowds got to know and they went after him. He made them welcome and talked to them about the kingdom of God; and he cured those who were in need of healing (Lk 9:11).

In short, he was tired of mobs and tried to get away, but when he saw the people, their suffering broke down his resolve. So he talked to them and healed them in spite of his weariness.

He knew so clearly that a central part of his mission was to go among the suffering, especially the poor, and to heal them. More often than we realize, Jesus is putting his fingers into the ears of a deaf man and saying, "Be opened"; putting mud cakes on the eyes of a blind man and telling him to wash in a pool; or simply saying the words, "Your faith has healed you." The leaders who were

Interested in discussion (the scribes and Pharisees) had to leave the big city of Jerusalem and try to find him in the hills, in the middle of the crowds who were clustered around him, grasping for healing.

...His fame spread thoughout Syria, and those who were suffering from diseases and painful complaints of one kind or another, the possessed, epileptics, the paralyzed, were all brought to him, and he cured them (Mt 4:24).

When you consider how much time Jesus spent praying with people, there had to be a reason for it.

The reason was simple: Jesus came to our fallen, wounded humanity to save and free us in every way. His Father—and ours —saw how miserable we were, in what sin, in what sickness, in what pain. Having compassion, he sent his only Son, Jesus, who was like us in every respect (except sin)—someone who understood us and our pain because he himself shared it. But there was one big difference: Because he was the Son of God he had the *power* in himself to change things.

He could forgive sins and heal sickness. "Everyone in the crowd was trying to touch him because power came out of him that cured them all" (Lk 6:19). Whenever sick people reached out to him he, in turn, reached out to them and their sickness disappeared.

He did all this because his mission was to save us and rescue us from the miserable state we were in: It was the very reason he came. When John the Baptist sent his followers to ask Jesus if he were the Messiah, Jesus simply showed that he was carrying out his saving mission:

> Go back and tell John what you have seen and heard: the blind see again, the lame walk, lepers are cleansed, and the deaf hear, the dead are raised to life, the Good News is proclaimed to the poor and happy is the man who does not lose faith in me (Lk 7:22-23).

Jesus wasn't boasting or trying to prove some point about being divine; he was just carrying out his work, the work of the savior of the human race. He loved people. He saw them as his brothers and sisters, and he couldn't

kingdom of God is at hand!" Life, health and love. The kingdom of Satan is being destroyed! Death, sickness and hate.

Can you see how much Jesus loved people? How much his heart went out to the sick? How he spent hours making his way through crowds and touching foul, leprous sores, even when it was against the law of his day to touch lepers? He really did care for us. He even healed on the Sabbath, straightening up a woman who had been bent over for 18 years (Lk 13:10-17), when it meant that the religious leaders would turn on him. One more day wouldn't have been intolerable, but he wasn't about to let her suffer even one more day.

Now, if that was part of his daily schedule, going out into the reeking crowds every day to touch and heal them 2000 years ago, do you think he is any less willing to do it today? At the Last Supper he told his followers that things were going to be better for them after he left, after he died and rose from the dead, because then the Spirit would be sent to empower them to do the same deeds that he himself had done (Jn 14:12) — and even greater deeds. He was going to live on in us and, by the power of the Spirit, would continue to heal in the 20th century as he had in the first.

Some Christians find it hard to believe that Jesus still wants to heal them in extraordinary ways, that healing is meant to be as ordinary, as frequent, as it was when Jesus walked out through the crowds every day in the glaring hot sun of Galilee.

You already know this just by studying the life and words of Jesus, especially in the Gospel of Luke. But you can also see it for yourself if you pray and ask Jesus to heal your friends and members of your family.

Just in the past six weeks alone I have seen five extraordinary cases of feet that were crippled and smaller than the normal foot,

was not psychosomatic; a real bone growth
had to take place for the changes to take
place. In one instance, it took only 10
minutes; in another it took two hours.

But what a wonderful thing: to see God's
healing power at work under our very eyes!
I didn't always have so much belief in the will-
ingness of Jesus to answer my prayers, but I
have now seen so much it would be hard for
me not to believe.

Step one in learning to pray with people
is to believe that Jesus is still at work healing
his people today. You will see marvelous
evidence of this if you just put into practice
the few simple things I will suggest in this
book.

Know that Jesus loves you and that he
has both the desire and the power to heal
you. *Believe* it and in time you will *ex-*

perience it. Finally, you will *know* it with a certainty that no one can shake: Jesus loves you and wants to heal his beloved people.

Two

Through You

It has been easy for me to believe that God is still willing to heal people in extraordinary ways through prayer. To encourage my faith I used to read eagerly the lives of holy people and the stories of God's wonderful works. It strengthened my faith to hear stories of how God still worked in our day. One book I read with fascination was Dr. Alexis Carrel's *Voyage to Lourdes*. Dr. Carrel was a skeptical physician who wanted to go to Lourdes with a trainload of sick people in order to gather evidence of the Catholic church's cruelty in building up the unrealistic

hopes of the sick, crowding them into train
cars (this was in the early 1900s) and making
them suffer the bouncing of the railroad on a
fruitless quest for healing. Once he got on the
crowded train he was asked to administer
morphine to a woman dying of tuberculosis of
the peritoneum. To Dr. Carrel she
represented exactly the kind of suffering patient who should be spared the pain of being
carted off to Lourdes, where he judged she
would probably die. Lourdes to him was not
hope for the sick; instead, it represented
cruelty and superstition. The tubercular
woman, however, survived the trip, was ex-
amined by the doctors of the Medical Bureau,
and then was wheeled out for the blessing of
the sick. Dr. Carrel stayed close to her to
alleviate her suffering with morphine, but also
because he expected to watch her die, right
there at Lourdes. Then he could write it up in
a Paris journal and expose Lourdes for the
mockery he saw it to be.

But wonder of wonders, at the blessing
of the sick, he saw her distended abdomen
flatten right down; he took her pulse and

temperature and found them to be normal.
Afterward, the doctors at the Medical Bureau
checked her and could find no trace of the
disease.

Dr. Carrel was honest enough to write up
his account, the reverse of what he had
originally intended. Yet, because he was
afraid of what his medical colleagues would
think, he signed his little book "Dr. Lerrac"
(Carrel spelled backward), so that no one but
his friends would guess that he wrote it.

That was the kind of book I used to
devour, for it encouraged me in my faith. The
problem was that I seldom saw anything like
that myself; it always seemed to occur in a
far-off place like France. Like so many Christians—Catholic, Orthodox and Protestant—I
didn't expect Jesus to work such wonders
through me. Mary, the mother of Jesus, was
holy and could intercede for us at the shrine
of Lourdes, but I had no right to expect much
to happen when I prayed. I believed in healing, but not *through me:* "Lord, I am not
worthy."

Is this true of you? If your husband is

sick, do you believe that God could heal him through your prayer? If your daughter is sick, would you have any confidence that you might lay your hands on her and see her restored to health?

Part of the Good News is that God wants to use your words and the touch of your hands to heal your loved ones. Even if you do not feel worthy or holy, Jesus wants to use you to pray for the needs in your family and your community.

The entire New Testament shows Jesus trying to *share* his powers with his followers. When Jesus looked at the crowds and had compassion on them because they were like sheep without a shepherd (Mt 9:36-38), he prayed that the Lord of the Harvest would send other laborers to reap the harvest. Even though he was the Son of God he did not want to do it alone; he needed help. Because his work included healing, he shared his healing power with human beings. He didn't reserve it to himself.

Cure the sick, raise the dead, cleanse the lepers, cast out devils (Mt 10:8).

Later, when the twelve were no longer enough to go to all the cities and villages, he chose 72 others and shared with them the very same powers (Lk 10:1-12). Now, the twelve were specially chosen, apostles, foun-dations of the church, forerunners of the bishops and leaders to come in future ages, but the seventy-two seem to have been appointed just for the task and later disappear from view—reminiscent of the 72 elders appointed to help Moses when he was overburdened (Nm 11:11ff.). The seventy-two seem to stand for ordinary people like us.

Later, when the Spirit descended upon all Christians at Pentecost, it was to empower the *entire* Christian community to perform the works that Jesus did: "These are the signs that will be associated with believers: . . . they will lay their hands on the sick who will recover" (Mk 16:17-18).

Do you see how clear the progression is?
1)   Jesus comes, sent by the Father, empowered to free and heal his people. He alone is our savior.

2) He shares his mission and his power with the twelve.

3) The needs of the people are over-whelming, so he shares his mission and power with the seventy-two.

4) At Pentecost he shares that mission and that power of the Spirit with *all the people* (although aspects of leadership and authority are reserved for Peter and the twelve), including the generations that are to come.

That includes *you.* You, who are reading this right now, are empowered by Jesus to pray for people, to heal the sick. The main condition is that you be Christian, although it is also important that you have received the empowering of the Spirit through confirmation or the baptism of the Spirit.[1] If you launch out, God will use you even now as you pray

1. The relationship of the sacrament of confirmation with the baptism of the Spirit is a much-discussed topic, but there is no need to go into it here. I do know that God has used the prayers of little children who are baptized but not confirmed to heal their parents. Yet, there also seems an added power to minister and heal that comes with confirmation or the baptism of the Spirit.

with your family and friends ... and the larger
world as well.

It is so important for you to know that
Jesus needs your prayers, in spite of your
weakness. You are not being proud or making yourself out as someone special if you
start to pray for the sick; you are just acting as
a normal Christian should.

When I first began to pray with people,
spiritual inferiority was my main problem, too.
I felt as if I were putting on an act, especially
since no one else that I was closely associated
with was praying with people. I was afraid of
looking ridiculous or being labeled as overly
pious. It may be that way with you, too. You
are going to have to get over your fear of
seeming different. I find that even husbands
and wives are afraid to pray with each other.

All these fears have robbed us of what
Jesus bequeathed to all his followers. How
otherwise can we explain why most Christian
fathers and mothers seldom pray with their
children?

But when you finally do get the courage
to pray — simply in obedience to God's

word, if for no other reason — you will discover in a real way that Jesus hears your prayers. You will never want to turn back. If you have never done this, have never prayed with someone before, you may resist what I am saying here. But once you have prayed several times and seen how wonderfully Jesus answers you, you will regret all the years you have missed praying with your friends. You will be like the seventy-two who came back rejoicing because they had seen the marvelous results of their prayer: " 'Lord,' they said, 'even the devils submit to us when we use your name' " (Lk 10:17).

No matter how weak you may feel as a Christian, no matter how lacking in the ability to create a beautiful prayer, it makes no difference. God hears the prayers of the little ones. "We are only the earthenware jars that hold this treasure, to make it clear that such an overwhelming power comes from God, and not from us" (2 Cor 4:7). Unworthiness is common to us all. All that counts is Jesus telling us to have confidence: "Ask and you shall receive." But moving from the realization

of books is actually starting to pray with people
is so difficult. You are afraid of intruding, of
asking something different, so you hold back. How
can you get started?

All I know is that I had to start one day
in a simple way. I just began to ask people,
"Would you like me to pray with you about
that?" To my surprise, they almost all said,
"Yes." Even the skeptics said: "I've got
nothing to lose. If you believe that God can
help, go ahead." I try to present the invitation
in a simple, quiet way, so that people won't
feel pushed into something. I ask in such a
way that they can easily say, "No," if they
don't want me to pray. But almost always
they say, "Yes."

Asking the people closest to you to pray
—your husband or your wife, for instance—
is often the hardest, because their "No" would
be a painful rejection. But that's part of the
life of a Christian, and we will never begin
unless we ask. We receive from God if we
ask, and we can only receive from our fellow
human beings, too, if we ask.

The reward is so great! It's not just that

prayers are answered—as they are. It's also
that I seldom love other people so deeply in a
real, non-possessive way, as when I pray for
them and see them change right before me.
And I seldom experience the love others have
for me as much as when I break down, con-
fess my own weakness and admit to my
friends that I need their prayers.

On the days when I don't pray with my
wife for the life I need that day, something is
really missing. I experience an aching
vacuum. This is not something I have been
taught; it is just a reality. I need the prayers of
the people closest to me to survive, just as I
need some time of solitary prayer. It's like the
emptiness many people feel when they are
used to receiving the Lord in the Eucharist
and then, some morning, they miss receiving.
So it is with the joined prayer of loved ones.
If you haven't experienced it, you can't realize
what you are missing. Even Jesus seemed to
need it; what else explains the disappointment
he felt in Gethsemane when he came back,
after his solitary agony, to his three closest
friends and found them asleep?

I find that even in those Christian groups
that believe in prayer for healing, there is a
tendency to depend too much on the celebrity
healer and the big healing service. I think it is
a wonderful thing to have healing services,
but not at the expense of praying at home for
the sick. Just recently I had a chance to check
with a group of 600 people the day after they
took part in a healing service where many
were prayed for. Of the 600, six said they
were totally healed and another 25 were improved. Now, it was wonderful that about 1%
were totally healed and another 4% were improved, but I believe that about 75% could be
totally healed or improved if we could spend
the time praying in small groups of friends.
Right now, I am part of a small group that
meets every Wednesday night and prays for
two hours for the sick among us; *most* of the
sick are visibly changed each week as we
pray. Occasionally someone is totally healed,
but mostly it's gradual—like Marianne, a nine-
year-old girl who is profoundly retarded and
whose body doesn't move properly as a result
of an overdose of flu vaccine, administered

when she was three. Five times now she has been to the prayer sessions and three of those five times her parents observed a change, either then or in the following week. Two weeks ago she was able to lift her leg in her first step since the overdose. A feeble step, certainly, and with Marianne being held up and supported by her father, but it was a step, the first in six years. As she took it, the group gathered around and applauded; we were so happy to see hope reborn in her parents as they saw the Lord at work in their daughter.

The same thing can happen as you learn the truth that will set you free: Jesus wants to use *your* prayers to bless and heal people. You don't have to be special—just an ordinary Christian, aware of your own weakness, or what you consider your own lack of faith.

Jesus wants to heal *through you*.
He will if you just give him the chance.

Three

Praying With People

Once you discover that God really answers you when *you* pray, the next step is for you to learn to pray *with* people, as well as *for* them, at a distance. For many years I prayed for people at a distance: A name would go up on the bulletin board, and later I would pray when I was alone in the chapel or in my room. That is a good way of praying. I still pray that way often, especially after someone has written a letter, asking for prayer; after all, Jesus cured the centurion's servant at a distance without bothering to travel to his home.

But when a friend asks you for prayer face to face, the most natural thing is to pray right then and there, on the spot. It used to be that when someone would ask me to pray, I would make a promise, "I'll remember you in my prayers," but I never thought of stopping to pray with him. No one had ever directly discouraged me from praying with people, yet, strange as it may seem, it never crossed my mind to do so. To me prayer was a private thing, except for the public prayers of the church. I would have been embarrassed to make up a prayer for someone; talking to God was too personal a thing to do with someone listening to me.

The strange thing is that, although there is no teaching that I know of in any church that would discourage Christians from praying spontaneously with one another, most Christians from mainline churches simply do not pray with each other in their own words. This is a special loss when we find that families do not feel comfortable praying together. Nor do priests or ministers, by and large (with the ex-

Praying With People

...tion of grace at meals), pray with each
other in their own words.

Some of our relationships to pray probably
goes back to our fear of revealing our inmost
thoughts and feelings to one another. I
remember vividly one meeting of theologians
in Rome in 1975. Father Kilian McDonnell,
O.S.B., shared with this distinguished group
that he once thought the charismatic renewal
was not for him personally because it was
overly emotional, even though it was a great
help to many people. Later, he continued, he
came to realize that that was simply a pitiful
excuse. The real reason he had difficulty was
that the renewal was *too personal.*

I think that is the trouble with most of us
in the beginning: We are locked up inside
ourselves and need to be formal and imper-
sonal in our religious observances. We are
afraid to pray out loud in somebody's
presence. I, for one, was certainly afraid of
being ridiculed for appearing pious. Several
times my father indicated to me that he would
like me to pray for his health, but I could not

bring myself to do it until near his death in the hospital's intensive care unit. Just thinking of it I could feel myself blush with embarrassment. The block was not on his part; he was a gentle man, who really wanted me to pray with him.

So, we need to be set free, to be given permission to pray with each other. When I am talking to a room full of people I can suggest that they try praying with one another right then and there and get over that initial fear. But since you are probably reading this book alone, all I can do is encourage you to pray with the people closest to you whenever the next natural opportunity comes up—for instance, when your child is sick, pray with the child and ask your husband or wife to join you.

What advantage is there in praying with someone when the Lord can help people at a distance? Well, there does seem to be an additional *power* that is there—I can tell you that from experience. Perhaps it's because the person you are praying with can hear your prayer, and that builds up his life or her faith. Perhaps it's the touch of your hand through which the power of God flows in a tangible way. Also, there seems to be a special presence of God when several people are gathered together in love.

> I tell you solemnly once again, if two of you
> on earth agree to ask anything at all, it will
> be granted to you by my Father in heaven.
> For where two or three meet in my name, I
> shall be there with them (Mt 18:19-20).

Most of the instantaneous, dramatic healings I have seen take place have been when there was a large gathering of Christian people, all praising God. God really does seem to dwell in the praises of his people, so I prefer to pray together with someone else, whenever possible. I have not only gotten over most of my fear, but I enjoy being with people when we pray so that I can see what's happening and talk with the person and find out how best to pray.

Most of all, when we pray with one another, we sense the love of Jesus, the sure sign of his presence. Once I was asked to pray for a 60-year-old sister who was going to the hospital the next day for an operation on the brain. At that time her community members were not familiar with praying for healing spontaneously as a group, but they gathered around to join me in praying. As we finished, her face was radiant and streaked with tears, as she said, "I have never before experienced the love of my community as deeply as I have tonight."

My prayer for you is that, as you pray with your loved ones, you come to know the love and the healing power of Jesus more deeply than ever before.

Four

Touch

Once you learn to pray *with* your friends, you will begin to understand why the New Testament lays such great stress upon touching people when you pray—the laying on of hands. "These are the signs that will be associated with believers: . . . they will lay their hands on the sick who will recover" (Mk 16:17-18). If I had been Mark, writing that section of the Gospel, I would probably have written "they will pray for the sick," rather than "they will lay their hands on the sick," but Mark and the other disciples realized that, even without words, there is a healing power in just touching another person. A mother demonstrates this when she picks up her crying child and holds it close and kisses away the hurt. She knows intuitively that her holding the child comforts and soothes it.

But, deeper than that, when you touch as well as pray for the other person, something else happens. In addition to the soothing, a *power* or gentle current often goes out from your hand to assist in the healing. Jesus was well aware of this. Once when he was in a crowd a woman suffering from an issue of blood decided that if she could just touch his clothes she would be healed. So she sneaked around in the crowd until she could touch him, and instantly the bleeding stopped. (She was doing all this secretively because, according to the law, a woman bleeding in this way was unclean, and she was afraid Jesus wouldn't break the law and touch her.) But Jesus, knowing he had been touched, looked around in the crowd and said, "Who touched my clothes?" He was aware that *"power had gone out from him"* (Mk 5:25-34).

Another time St. Luke records that
everyone in the crowd was trying to touch
him because power came out of him that
cured them all (Lk 6:19). It wasn't only
Jesus who seemed to emanate this kind of
life-giving power. His followers did, too. The
people used to lay their sick out in the streets
hoping that Peter's shadow might fall across
them (Acts 5:15), and others would take
handkerchiefs that Paul had touched and use
them for healing the sick and casting out evil
spirits (Acts 19:11-12).

In short, the early Christians had a lively
sense of healing and the power of touch.
Now, you definitely are not Peter or Paul, so
you may think it prideful to claim to have
some significant spiritual power in your hands.
I know, because I certainly felt that way
myself when I first began to pray *with* people
instead of just *for* them. But remember, the
Gospel of Mark (16:17) says that one of the
signs that will follow *believers,* not just holy
people, is that they will lay their hands on the
sick who will recover.

As a Christian you also know that the

Father, the Son and the Holy Spirit dwell within you. This is a traditional belief of Christians, taken from the last discourse of Jesus in St. John (chapters 14-17). The life of the Trinity is within you; that life of God within you (sanctifying grace in Catholic terminology) is a gift and no credit on your part, but it should have an effect on other people if you let it burn brightly.

Nearly every day I see this communication of life from one person to another take place. When we lay our hands upon sick people, they almost always experience *heat*. It's not an ordinary heat that just touches the surface of the skin but one that seems to search deep into whatever organ has been affected by sickness. (Occasionally, the reverse happens: Persons suffering from overheating in the joints due to arthritis experience coolness when we lay hands upon their knees or fingers.) Furthermore, I, for one, have a low body temperature, so my skin temperature is usually cooler than that of the person I am praying for (especially if he has a fever). It seems as if the heat is caused by the sick per-

can radiate light and life to everyone around
you. If you believe the common teaching of
Christianity—that God lives within you—you
should find it easy to see that your touch can
heal! That doesn't make you an extraordinary
Christian, a saint. It just means that you are
an ordinary Christian. This is in itself extraordinary!

In fact, I know several people who were
healed just by being looked at. They experienced the presence of Jesus coming
through a Christian's eyes, and it was enough
to heal them. Nor should this surprise us. If
we can be infected with sickness by getting
near sick people, why shouldn't we be
touched by life and health when we draw
close to the source of life, Jesus?

So, if you have never prayed with someone and put your hand upon them while you
prayed, I encourage you to try it. If your child

is sick, laying your hand upon the child is such a natural thing to do anyway. It should be just as natural to pray for a husband, wife or friend—once you get over that initial shyness. Holding a person's hand or putting your arm around a shoulder is such a natural gesture. If the person is sick and it can be done decently, put your hand near the affected area while you are praying.

If you do start praying with people, you should soon see enough healings take place through your touch to encourage you and strengthen your faith even more.

For instance, you may pray with a person who has a tumor and, as you put your hand upon that tumor, you may gradually see it disappear. At first, you won't be sure: Is it just your imagination? But then, as you pray, you find, to your amazement, that it really is shrinking. Usually, it just takes one or two experiences like that to convince you that God still wants ordinary people like you—simple believers—to lay hands upon the sick who will then recover.

There is one beautiful discovery about

healing touch, that I would especially like to
share, and that is how wonderful it is for a
husband (or friends) to pray for a pregnant
wife and her unborn baby. Sometimes the
baby gives its first kick as the mother is prayed
for — life responding to life. Of course, if the
mother is alone she can put her hand upon
her stomach and pray for the child. A friend,
Dr. Conrad Baars, says that a mother can actually play with her unborn child by placing
her hand, first on one side for a while, then
on the other. The baby will turn in the womb,
gradually shifting around until its back is
toward the mother's loving hand. Parents who
have prayed for their children before birth
report that these children seem to be happier,
cry less and have better dispositions than their
children born in previous years without such
prayer. It's something like John the Baptist
being touched in Elizabeth's womb when

1. When I have checked this out in church congregations by
a show of hands, I have found that only a tiny number of
parents have ever prayed in this way for children before birth.
It would be wonderful if pastors would teach parents such
simple, positive ways of praying.

The Prayer That Heals

Mary, bearing Jesus, came to visit: "Now as soon as Elizabeth heard Mary's greeting, the child leaped in her womb and Elizabeth was filled with the Holy Spirit" (Lk 1:41). This biblical scene reminds me of a healing seminar in Tulsa when we prayed with a pregnant mother: At that very moment she felt her child leap as she herself was filled with the Spirit! What could be a more beautiful and natural scene than a husband and wife praying together for their unborn child!

Five

In Your Own Words

For many years I was hesitant about making up a prayer in my own words; no one had ever encouraged me to do so. The prayers I said were memorized prayers like the "Our Father." Certainly it is good to memorize prayers as a child and to use them as an adult, but we have many specific needs that can best be voiced by specific prayer.

Jesus and his disciples felt free to make up prayers that suited the need of the moment. So far as I know neither Jesus nor his followers repeated the same prayer twice when praying with people; they simply spoke to God as we speak to one another. Prayer is a heart-to-heart conversation with God who loves us. In our ordinary conversation with friends we don't write speeches or repeat what was said last time. Even the "Our Father" does not seem to have been memorized word for word in the same way by all the early Christian communities, for Matthew and Luke have different versions of it. The version we memorize is from Matthew (6:9-13), but Luke's version is much shorter:

> Father, may your name be held holy,
> your kingdom come;
> give us each day our daily bread,
> and forgive us our sins,
> for we ourselves forgive each one who is in
> debt to us.
> And do not put us to the test (Lk 11:1-4).

Luke, then, seems concerned about the main drift of the Lord's prayer and not about a word-for-word memorization.

The apostles, too, were free in making up their own prayers to suit the person they were praying with. For instance, Peter said to a paralytic: "Aeneas, Jesus Christ cures you:

get up and hold up your sleeping mat" (Acts 9:34). To the lame man at the Gate Beautiful, Peter said, "I have neither silver nor gold, but I will give you what I have. In the name of Jesus Christ the Nazarene, walk!" (Acts 3:6).

I could give countless other examples; the point is simply that the followers of Jesus felt free to make up prayers to suit the needs of the people they were praying with. On the other hand, many Christians from mainline churches have become so used to formal, memorized prayers that they are afraid of launching out and becoming personal about their faith in public.[1] Perhaps the fear is of appearing pious. Perhaps it is the fear of making a mistake in a church group where doc-

---

1. It is significant, I think, that in the United States most mainline Protestant churches are either losing members or just holding steady, while Pentecostal and Evangelical churches, where the personal expression of faith is encouraged, are growing rapidly. (The Roman Catholic Church has a slow growth in numbers which is roughly equivalent to the population growth.) A good case can be made that where Christians do not experience a personal relationship with Jesus Christ, they will have little desire to share their faith with others—or to pray with others.

trine has been emphasized. In any case, many Christians seldom voice a personal prayer, except for an occasional grace at meals. Men especially are afraid of "emotionalism" and use that as an excuse not to pray in a personal way.

Yet, no church teaches against voicing your own prayer, and it is a most natural thing to do—a Christian heritage of which our fears have robbed us. When you do pray from the heart in your own words it is a most beautiful thing. I remember one of the first times I ever heard someone pray in his own words. It was during the first "cursillo" held in Iowa in the early 60s. One night a few of us had gone into the chapel and a burly truck driver began praying to Jesus in his own words about the mess he felt he had made of his life, and all of us in the room began to weep. For years we had all said this kind of prayer privately, but to hear an ordinary person, a truck driver, open up his heart was something I had never heard before. So there I was, more than 30 years old, hearing a spontaneous prayer for the first time.

Aside from getting rid of our fears, making up a prayer should be easy. It's as easy as talking to someone who is our friend, for Jesus has assured us that we are his friends. He has encouraged us over and over to ask his Father for anything, according to his will, and it will be granted.

> We are quite confident that if we ask him for
>   anything,
> and it is in accordance with his will,
> he will hear us;
> and, knowing that whatever we may ask, he
>   hears us,
> we know that we have already been granted
>   what we asked of him (1 Jn 5:14-15).

He told us not to babble or make up long prayers—all we need to do is voice a simple prayer from the heart.

There are several ways that you can pray for healing. For instance, some Christians who are specially close to Jesus and who can sense when he wants to heal a particular person, can say a prayer of *command*, just as Jesus commanded the waves and wind to die down and Peter commanded the lame man to walk. Since the kingdom of God involves restoring everything to its proper order, the Christian has an authority to pray the prayer of command. The forces of nature, then, must obey when this prayer is backed by the authority of God. At times, for example, I pray a prayer of command for cancer patients: "In the name of Jesus Christ I command these cancer cells to wither up and die. I command these tumors to shrink up and dissolve. From now on let nothing but normal cells be reproduced in this body. In the name of Jesus I command this cancer to leave this body that it may be whole."

Now to say that kind of prayer of command demands that you have a sure sense of what God wants, and it may sound beyond the confidence that most of us can muster when we are learning to pray.

What you can easily do, though, is simply to *ask* God for what you want: "Jesus, please send your healing power into my wife's body and kill the cancer cells. Dissolve the tumors and fill her with new strength. Give the command that normal, healthy cells be

produced by her body from now on. I and
please heal my wife and restore her to full
health. That kind of prayer should be easy to
make up — simply speak to God what is in
your heart, with no pretense. You know he
loves you, so just talk to him as a friend.

Somehow we have the idea that we have
to make up an elaborate prayer to impress
God, that if our prayer is ordinary God won't
hear it. But that's not true. You don't have to
pray in King James English; just speak the
way you would to a friend. Nor do you have
to pray in some tone of voice different from
the tone you would use speaking to a friend
at dinner. Be yourself when you pray—with
no artificiality. "In your prayers do not babble
as the pagans do, for they think that by using
many words they will make themselves
heard" (Mt 6:7).

Your prayer in English need not be more
than a few minutes long. If you are accus-
tomed to pray in tongues that can be a help,
too. The way I usually pray is to pray in
English for a little bit and then pray in tongues
for as long as I feel it's helpful while keeping

my hand upon the person's shoulder or other affected part. By praying in tongues I am turning the prayer over to the Holy Spirit who understands, far better than I, what is best to pray for. The prayer, then, rises above the limitations of my understanding of the situation. On at least three occasions while I was praying in tongues, the person I was praying with heard me praying in a language he or she understood and I didn't (in one instance, Arabic; in another, Greek). They all found the experience very helpful—and encouraging (in two of the instances the persons were not charismatic and were skeptical about tongues previous to the actual prayer).

But I don't want to belabor the benefit of praying in tongues. You can pray in English—or whatever your native language is—in the most simple, natural way, and the Lord will respond to your prayer.

Ask, and it will be given to you; search and you will find; knock and the door will be opened to you (Lk 11:9).

Six

It Takes Time

One of the great discoveries in my life has been that when a short prayer doesn't seem to help, a "soaking " prayer often brings the healing we are looking for. Over and over I have checked the effect of prayer by asking groups how many were *totally healed* when we prayed a short prayer and how many were *improved*. The number of people who experience some real improvement usually outnumbers those who are totally healed by five to one. This led me to realize that a short prayer usually has some physical effect (and always a spiritual effect) upon a person, but

that most of us need to take more time when
we pray for the sick.

Just last night I prayed with about 15
people and two or three seemed completely
healed, but the majority experienced improvement. The longer we prayed, the better they
felt. One was a secretary whose fingers were
tightening up with arthritis, a frightening pros-
pect, since it could mean the loss of her job.
The week before, when we prayed, about half
the stiffness left. Last night, to her great
delight, it almost disappeared! The time element seems to be essential; the straightening
of her fingers took two sessions of prayer.
Other times it takes much longer.

Many healings could take place in your
family prayer if you simply could spend time
with one another, praying in the simple ways
I have mentioned. Suppose your elderly
father has arthritis, especially in the spine and
fingers. If you pray with him in your own
words and simply ask Jesus—or the
Father—to heal him, and then hold his fingers
in your hands or put your hand upon his back

and continue to pray in silence ¹ or pray in tongues, or sing gently (whatever seems right to you), you may also very well see a change take place before your eyes. This usually takes place in stages, as the following are things to look for:

First, the *pain* will diminish and, perhaps, completely go away in the course of about 10 minutes (sometimes more, sometimes less).

Next, look for a return of *mobility* and flexibility. Ask him to move his fingers, or bend his spine and see if it is more flexible. This usually takes longer.

Last, if he has *swellings* on the joints you may see the swelling go down and the gnarled fingers start to straighten. (When I pray, this usually becomes visible in about half an hour.)

I want to encourage you by letting you know that these changes start to take place *most of the time* when we pray with arthritis patients. While I realize that God may have given me (and many others) a special gift in

1. Catholics might wish to pray the rosary.

praying for healing, still I believe that similar blessings will happen in your family if you pray. It may take a little longer, perhaps, but healing will often come while you pray. What I say here of arthritis you can apply to praying for other physical sicknesses.

At times I have had to pray for hours with one person until the healing was complete. You will find that it is work, but it is worth every moment, for it is such a delight to be able to bring God's healing to someone. Another person we prayed with last night, a young woman with scoliosis, was so happy, her face covered with tears of joy, because she could feel her spine straightening and the pain leaving while the prayer was going on.

There are different ways of spending time praying with someone. Sometimes I feel drawn to pray an hour or two with someone, with five-minute breaks at regular intervals to rest and check to see if any improvement has taken place.

I usually spend a longer time when there is no chance of seeing the person for some time, or when it is a very serious illness and

It's important that healing start as soon as
possible. Sometimes so much change and
healing is going on that it would be a pity to
stop.

In other cases, it seems best just to pray
five minutes at a time every day or every
week. This might be specially suitable for a
husband and his wife praying with each other
for any needs they may have. In any event,
having someone pray with you is such a
beautiful, strengthening experience that you
probably won't want the person or group
members to stop praying with you once they
have started. The one doing the praying, on
the other hand, may have to stop, because
prayer usually takes something out of you.
(About two hours' praying with people at a
healing service is my limit; after that I really
start to become exhausted.)

As I understand it, the time element of
soaking prayer is needed because so much
healing comes through *touch*. The longer the
sick area is held in the healing light of God,
the more the germs or tumors have to wither
up and die. I like to think of it as God's radia-

tion treatment. The life of God is transmitted through your hand, but it is not God's un-diminished life and power. It is his power all right, but it is filtered through your weakness and your brokenness. So, naturally, it takes time for it to take effect.

For families who have retarded children, or children with cerebral palsy, or who have any kind of serious, chronic sicknesses, soaking prayer is a wonderful thing. The instances that I personally know of mental retardation or brain damage being cured have all been through long-term prayer (over a period of years frequently), where the family really prayed with the child as a daily commitment. One of the beautiful effects is that the sick person always experiences God's love during the prayer, and this in itself is healing. You should also be aware that, with brain damage or ailments like that, the repair is beyond the power of nature; a real creative miracle by God is needed, rather than just an ordinary healing. I find that this kind of miracle occurs more rarely than healing. Occasionally it oc-c s instantly (usually at a large healing ser-

place where there is a special presence of God, but usually it takes place over a long period of time in a family dedicated to prayer.

Right now, for instance, our prayer group prays once a week with a profoundly retarded eight-year-old girl. Her parents are also praying with her every day. After two months of prayer with our group, she is still retarded, but every other week she improves in some tangible way. After last week's prayer, for instance, her eyes started to follow her parents' hand movements, something she had not been able to do before. We see steady progress that her therapists can verify; it seems to be taking place at a much faster pace than natural causes can account for—and yet the healing may take years.

But these gradual healings that take time are such a sign of hope. When I see a sick person now, my thought is, "If only someone could pray with that man in the wheelchair for several hours I believe he could walk." I hope you recognize the wonderful ability you have to transmit the life of Jesus to the people around you, how you can pray with your friends (or sometimes, strangers) and see their sickness swallowed up in life.

Even Jesus touched a blind man twice before he could see clearly (Mk 8:22-26), and he told us about "the need to pray continually and never lose heart" (Lk 18:1). So be encouraged if you have a loved one who is seriously ill; spend time with that person, pray frequently; lay your hands upon the person for five or more minutes and see if any change takes place. If change does take place, then be encouraged to pray longer, for as long as you both have strength.

If you begin to do this, if you are willing to get down to the work of praying and not settle for the "cheap grace" of an instant prayer, you will begin to see wonders take place as your loved ones grow in wisdom and grace and health.

Seven

Forgiveness

"Yes, if you forgive others their failings, your heavenly Father will forgive yours; but if you do not forgive others, your Father will not forgive your failings either" (Mt 6:14-15). Similarly, just as our Father will not forgive us, he will not heal us until we forgive those who have injured us.

Part of this is a natural spiritual law: We have all sinned and, as a sign that we believe God will forgive us out of his compassion and goodness, we must be willing to pass that forgiveness on to others and break the chain of hate that affects the whole human race. "It is the man who is forgiven little who shows little love" (Lk 7:47). We cannot receive the love of Jesus, the lifeblood that circulates through us and keeps us going, unless we are willing to pass it on to others. We need to change our hearts of stone into hearts of flesh.

The tragedy is that so many marriages and other relationships are poisoned and wounded. A mother says something unkind to her child, "It's too bad you are not as pretty as your sister," and 30 years later you may still find that insult rankling in an adult woman who is unsure about herself and finds it hard to trust. She felt betrayed by her mother, the one who was closest to her and knew her best, and the experience has affected her whole life. Or a husband may say something cutting to his wife who retorts in kind. Before you know it, there is a distance between them that tends to widen unless they forgive one another. "Bear with one another; forgive each other as soon as a quarrel begins" (Col 3:13).

So, a vital part of our prayer with one

another is talking out any differences that we
may have and expressing our feelings in a
constructive way. Then forgive one another
and pray for each other for any wounds you
may have inflicted. If you haven't already
discovered it, you will find that you cannot
pray in any real, spontaneous way with others
when you hold something against them or
believe that they have something against you.

So then, if you are bringing your offering to
the altar and there remember that your
brother has something against you, leave
your offering there before the altar, go and
be reconciled to your brother first, and then
come back and present your offering (Mt
5:23-24).

Over and over again I have seen people
physically healed once they were willing to
forgive someone who had hurt them! It's
amazing how we Christians are sensitive to
such sins as drunkenness and adultery, but
seem so insensitive to the hatred we may be

1. Here I would especially recommend reading *Feeling and
Healing Your Emotions* by Dr. Conrad Baars (Logos International).

constantly nourishing in our hearts. Usually we believe that the other person is really bad—or, at least, the person's action is—and he or she doesn't deserve anything but scorn and punishment. At the moment I write this, for instance, Iran is holding 53 hostages from the United States, and everywhere I go now I see bumper stickers that insult Iran and store signs that say "Iranians not welcome," or hear radios blaring forth a song attacking the Ayatollah and Iran. Now, the holding of the hostages is wrong, but some Christians don't seem to have any compunction about hating a whole group of the world's people. Hating at a distance may not be so dangerous, but holding grudges at home is devastating. It not only binds up the person we hate, but it can also bind us up and make us sick. When we hate or harbor anger, without working it out, we hurt ourselves even more than the other person. Our hate may eventually destroy us.

More and more, doctors are discovering the role that unresolved feelings play in making us sick. Dr. and Mrs. Carl Simonton in *Getting Well Again* (Bantam Books, Inc.)

show evidence that unresolved loss of habits
can lead to cancer's onslaught. Dr. James
Lynch in *The Broken Heart* (Harper & Row
Publishers, Inc.) gives evidence that lack of
love and community increases the incidence
of heart disease, and nearly everyone
recognizes that tension and anger building up
over a period of time can lead to certain kinds
of arthritis and ulcers.

Increasingly, then, medical people and
praying people are coming to the same con-
clusion: Sickness may be caused or ag-
gravated by unresolved emotions, especially
fear and anger. Ultimately we need to forgive,
to give up the grudges and resentments that
cause adrenalin and other endocrine secre-
tions to continuously pour into our bodily
systems, when these substances were only
meant to be secreted occasionally, to help us
during times of emergency. If I am afraid over
a period of time, my shoulders hunch up in a
fear reaction; if I am habitually afraid, I may
end up in a permanent stoop and my posture
will be permanently affected.

How much I need God's help to forgive,

especially my enemies! I truly believe that holding grudges is such a natural process that only Jesus can free us.[2] Often I have prayed with someone who was unable to forgive and have asked Jesus to fill the person with his own understanding and love for the other party and then to pour out his forgiving love into the heart of the person who is having a hard time forgiving. Over and over I have seen this prayer answered with the forgiveness that Jesus won upon the cross when he cried out, "Father, forgive them; they do not know what they are doing" (Lk 23:34).

At times the person you cannot forgive may be yourself. You may feel so guilty that you do not even want to be healed. You are punishing yourself. If this is true for you, it is

2. Because the Gospel speaks so much about forgiveness, many Christians feel guilty about feeling angry. Yet Jesus was very angry at times, as when he called the Pharisees a "brood of vipers." Paul says we should be angry but not sin. Anger is a good, God-given emotion. But we must choose an appropriate action to work out our anger and at the appropriate time, we must forgive. *Healing Life's Hurts* by Fathers Matt and Dennis Linn, S.J. (Paulist Press) is a fine book that shows how we can work through our anger to a point of forgiveness.

Many people can't *feel* forgiven, even when they *know* they are forgiven. For instance, a woman who has had an abortion may be unable to shake the feeling of guilt, even after repenting, for she knows that her child would be alive if she had not ended its life. That death doesn't change after repentance; something happened to that child and it cannot be changed. When something like this happens, the following approach to prayer is often helpful.

First, have the person imagine Jesus (or the Father) with the eyes of their spirit. (If you are praying alone, you can do this yourself.) Try to see Jesus as clearly as possible and speak to him. Listen to him, should he choose to speak. Or perhaps he will shake your hand or even embrace you. After you have welcomed Jesus in this way and are

71

comfortable, imagine him standing by your side. The door opens and the person with whom you need to be reconciled walks in. Try to see the person clearly: the expression on the face, the way the hair looks, the look in the eyes. Then, asking Jesus to help you, go up to that person and say or do whatever Jesus inspires you to do. Often this prayer comes alive in the Spirit. You really seem to see Jesus; he helps you by putting a true desire in your heart to be reconciled. You may end up asking for forgiveness or the other person may ask for yours; you may end up shaking hands or embracing; you may see Jesus with his arms around both of you; you may feel a great weight of resentment being lifted, almost physically, off your shoulders.

You can pray this kind of prayer, too, for a friend. I know of extraordinary things Jesus has done in freeing people of unforgiveness and guilt. For instance, I mentioned earlier that there is often need for a woman to forgive herself if she has undergone an abortion. There is also a need to ask forgiveness of the child for her action. Although the child

forgiveness

is physically dead, its spirit lives on and somewhere in God's universe that child still exists.

Once I prayed for a woman who wanted to be released from her feeling of guilt. She had gone to confession and asked God's forgiveness, but she still felt guilty. First, I suggested that she ask God to bring her the child, so that she might ask the child's forgiveness for ending its life. After I prayed for that she was silent for a long time and then she laughed. What she saw was this: God the Father appeared to her, holding the child. She was relieved to see that the child was happy. (Amazingly, the child was about two years old—the age the baby would have been if she had not had the abortion.) Then the child turned to her and smiled, and she knew that she was forgiven. Then the Father turned to her and smiled, and she felt, in that instant, the wonder of God's forgiveness. In this way she knew, totally, that God forgave her, her child forgave her, and she was finally able to forgive herself.

In this kind of prayer there is much

creativity—creativity on the level of God's inspiration, on the level of the story of the
Prodigal Son. So I encourage you to try it if
you are burdened by a soured relationship
that you know needs healing. Ask someone
to pray with you, or pray alone in the way I
have suggested.

If you still are in relationship with the
other person, you may need to make an effort to work out a reconciliation. Sometimes a
third party, such as a marriage counselor, is
needed. One suggestion I would make is this:
Ask for forgiveness with humility; offer
forgiveness with sensitivity. You can say: "I
am sorry I have sinned against you. I
shouldn't have done it. Forgive me, loose me,
free me."

But if you approach someone and say, "I
forgive you," it may sound as if you are taking a superior position and saying, "You have
sinned against me, but I am generous enough
to forgive you." Several times people have
told me unexpectedly that they forgave me,
and each time it sounded to me as if they
were trying to judge me, and let me know

what they thought in a rather sneaky way. For example, what would you think if someone came up to you and said, "You have always appeared to me to be proud and insensitive. I don't know if you are or not, but I shouldn't be judging just because you seem haughty to me. So I ask your forgiveness"?

That kind of statement might come as a shock to you, or make you angry. Here you are being asked to forgive a person for something you didn't even know about! If you need to forgive, the safest thing to do is to forgive quietly, in your heart. Say it out loud only when the other person actually asks for forgiveness.

On the other hand, it's actually best to take the initiative when you are guilty and ask for forgiveness. The other person may not give it, but you have done your part to be reconciled.

Sometimes a relationship suffers, not because you did something wrong, but because there is something missing—especially if that something is an expression of love and appreciation. I know that I never was

75

able to express my love for my mother and father adequately until their last days. If I had been able simply to say, "I love you," it would have made them so much happier.

I remember one woman with whom Sister Jeanne Hill and I prayed. She asked us to pray for the healing of her relationship with her father who had never showed her the love and affection she needed as his daughter. She had earlier received several beautiful inner healings, but after this prayer nothing seemed to happen. As she put it, she felt as if she were in a pressure cooker; the healing had not yet happened. It did not, in fact, take place until several days later when she went to visit her father. She let herself into the house and went to the living room where she saw her father as she had always seen him, watching TV, drinking beer, with his feet propped up on a stool. She was standing at the door, wondering whether or not to go in, when she seemed to hear a voice telling her to go to her dad and tell him that she loved him. At first she resisted, believing that he would only laugh at her. But the inner urging persisted until finally she overcame her reluctance, walked up to his chair, knelt down beside him and said, "Dad, I love you." For a few seconds her fears were realized as he kept staring ahead, watching the TV screen. Then he turned toward her, burst into tears and threw his arms around her. As they wept together, the healing of years of hurt took place.

Clearly, God was not satisfied until reconciliation had taken place not only in her heart, but in reality.

You probably know yourself how loving relationships can free you to be the kind of person you want to be, while hateful relationships bind you up. So do what you can to set others free. I now see a deeper meaning in "Whatever you bind on earth shall be bound in heaven; whatever you loose on earth shall be loosed in heaven."

Although Jesus addressed these words to Peter as he gave him authority in his apostolic band, there is a sense in which all of us can

bind and loose each other to do the work of
the kingdom. It is true: If you do not forgive,
you will not be forgiven or healed.

Over and over I have seen sick people
physically healed at the moment they were
able to forgive a long-standing enemy. In
Power to Heal (Ave Maria Press) I wrote
about the healing of Teresa's leg which had
been dreadfully warped and twisted by
osteomyelitis. On the second day of our
prayer the healing seemed to stop. At that
point we discovered that Teresa needed to
forgive her mother. When Teresa was injured
at the age of nine her mother, who was poor,
had to turn her over to a group of sisters who
could give Teresa the medical attention she
needed. Although her mother was doing what
she thought best, it seemed to Teresa that her
mother was abandoning her. She grew angry
and distant because of what she felt was rejection. When we asked Teresa to forgive her
mother—which she did—her leg started
straightening and growing once more.

To me it is such a mystery how tangled,
how wounded our relationships can become

the power to forgive those who have injured you.

Eight

The Faith to Be Healed

Unless you grew up in a pentecostal church, you probably belong to a Christian church where the minister and the people do not expect healing through prayer to take place as an everyday event. But then, if you became involved in a charismatic prayer group, you probably experienced a religious shock as you faced a nearly opposite belief: Unless you absolutely believe you are going to be healed when they pray for you, it is clear that you lack faith. There are leaders in some prayer

groups I have visited who believe in this way.
They won't be content unless you "lay claim
to your healing"—even if you still have the
symptoms of sickness after they have prayed.

Now, there are many good Christians
who have that absolute faith in healing and
they report many healings that take place
through their prayers. But if you have been
put off by their absolute demands, or if you
simply are being honest enough to say that
you are somewhat skeptical because you have
never seen any healing take place through
prayer, I want to encourage you not to lose
heart. A number of the people I have prayed
with and who were healed didn't seem to
have much belief at all, and some were not
even Christian. I remember a Buddhist monk
who somehow got into one of our retreats in
Japan. I had a long discussion with him one
night at table: To him Christ was a great man,
but only one among many in whom a spark
of the divine resided. But next night, when
we were praying for healing, he came forward
and he was mightily touched by God. I think

for one reason or another. I remember visiting
Lourdes in 1975 and speaking with the doctors at the Medical Bureau. They were
discussing the case of a man who had lost a
part of a bone during World War II and the
bone was restored during a visit to Lourdes.
The doctors were ready to certify the cure as
miraculous (a rare occurrence now—only
once every two or three years do the doctors
at Lourdes do this), but the church officials
were unwilling to ratify the cure because the
man's marital status was irregular. I find,
though, that Jesus heals and blesses people
today just as he did 2000 years ago, and that
he includes some whom we might judge un-
worthy of his attention.

Now you may believe that you don't
have the kind of faith that would enable Jesus
to say to you, "Your faith has healed you; go

in peace."[1] Perhaps you don't have a strong faith; perhaps you are even skeptical. You are not sure you will be healed of your illness, or that your prayers for someone else are worth very much.

That's all right; you have to start where you are. So, first of all, be honest. If you have just so much faith, God will work with that. I have seen just about as many people healed who were not sure what was going to happen, as those who were sure. To be sure that you are going to be healed requires a special revelation from God: that revelation is given to some, but not to everyone. The big thing is not to fake it. Just work with whatever belief you have. If God chooses to heal you, that will help increase your faith.

Healing does not always come *from* faith. Sometimes it leads *to* faith.

Secondly, our faith is in God, and the fact that he *does* heal. (In fact, his healing is

1. Dr. Charles Farah, Jr., has written a book on this subject, *From the Pinnacle of the Temple: Faith vs. Presumption* (Logos International), in which he goes into the dangers of identifying faith with a readiness to claim healing without a special inspiration from God.

factors. Ultimately, of course, in the city of God, "He will wipe away all tears from their eyes; there will be no more mourning or sadness" (Rv 21:4).

So what I want to encourage you to believe is this: *Ordinarily God wants to heal his people as soon as possible.* But there are a variety of reasons people are not healed when we pray, and they don't all reflect badly on the person who is sick.[2] Death, for instance, comes to us all. It is not the ultimate tragedy, but rather an entrance into new life. Agnes Sanford believes that her husband, who had suffered a stroke, was kept alive two years longer than necessary by well-meaning friends who kept praying for him and wouldn't let him go when, in God's perfect timing, he was ready to go.

2. In my book, *Healing* (Ave Maria Press), chapter 18 is a discussion of the reasons people are not healed.

If you have a lively belief in God's goodness and faith—that he is on the side of life and health and that he also has the *power* to bring us healing when everything we have done has failed—then you have the kind of faith that is sufficient to bring about healing. (Even if you don't have that much faith, pray with what you do have, and you will still find that wonderful things happen.) Just pray as honestly as you can, relax and expect to be surprised.

My experience leads me to believe that the kind of person who most often receives healing is someone who is open and receptive to goodness and love and truth. I have seen a kind of bright-eyed look, the look of a child, and when I see it, I usually sense that the person will be healed. Sometimes you see that look of a child in an 80-year-old woman; sometimes you see it in a college student. Somehow that open kind of person seems to receive healing most often. The person who has a harder time receiving healing is a controlled person who has to think everything through before acting, a person who is filled

God—is hard for them.

This openness to receive healing seems to have a lot to do with what Jesus said about becoming like a little child if we wish to enter the kingdom of God (Mt 19:13-15). I think there are people who do not know Jesus yet (like the Roman centurion Cornelius in Acts 10), but who have a readiness of heart to trust and believe and, in my experience, they are the ones most often healed. You can see it in their eyes.

So become like a little child. Don't try to figure out too much. Do not strain. Just be obedient and pray with your friends, and you will find that God is much better than you thought he was!

> Is there a man among you who would hand his son a stone when he asked for bread? Or would hand him a snake when he asked for a fish? If you, then, who are evil, know how

to give your children what is good, how
much more will your Father in heaven give
good things to those who ask him! (Mt
7:9-11).

Nine

The Love That Heals

The great healing evangelists with special gifts usually emphasize the kind of *faith* that heals. Their gifts, such as knowing when people are being healed and encouraging them to "claim their healing" may intimidate ordinary people. You may think you have to imitate them or you may just give up and say to yourself, "I don't have that kind of faith, so there's no point in my praying." Or perhaps you are tempted to think that those evangelists are overemotional and that they are making extravagant claims.

But you, as an ordinary person, don't have to pray like that. As I said in the last chapter, your faith can simply be in God's goodness: He loves this person you are praying for more than you do; what he wants is best, and that probably means he wants to heal him. He loves you enough to listen to your prayers and to answer them. So stress love in praying with members of your family and you can't go wrong.

Several things happen if you pray and concentrate on God's love for you and for your family and friends. First, if you are a loving person, many of your own sicknesses will be taken care of, and you will be healthier. More and more doctors are discovering the relationship between our inner spiritual state and the health of our bodies. For instance, some doctors now say that the basic source of heart attack is a distortion of spiritual values that causes us to be too competitive, to value work more than people and to race the clock. That kind of behavior, Type A behavior,[1] sets

1. A fascinating book on this subject, *Type A Behavior and Your Heart* by Doctors Friedman and Rosenman (Fawcett-Crest), is excellent reading if you have had heart problems or if you are the typically American competitive type of person.

Second, if you sense the love of God for

you and the person you pray for, you will be
gentle. You can relax ("Why are you so anxious, O you of little faith?"); you can speak in
a quiet voice and your prayers will be gentle.
You won't need to imitate those who speak in
powerful voices or who shout and strain. You
can speak to God in the same tone of voice
as you would to a friend, with the quiet confidence that he will hear and answer you. If
you have a friend who loves you, you know
you don't need to argue with that person or
use a loud voice; all you need to do is tell
your friend what you need, and you know he
will do everything possible to help. So it is
with Jesus. They said of Jesus, "He will not
brawl or shout, nor will anyone hear his voice
in the streets. He will not break the crushed
reed, nor put out the smouldering wick . . ."
(Mt 12:19-20). He appreciates the gentle
prayer that shows confidence in his friendship

more than a raised voice. In short, when you pray with your family, you can use the same tone of voice speaking to God that you use in speaking to them. You can just relax and be yourself.

Third, you will sense more than ever that somehow the life and love of Jesus flow into people when you lay your hands on them. Just as babies need to be held or they may develop a sickness or even wither up and die, so we wither up spiritually and die without the infilling of God's love, which ordinarily comes to us through other people. If you truly understand that, you will be willing to spend time praying with people, sensing that something of the life and love of Jesus comes through your hand to touch and to heal.

How well I remember a priest in my community who was dying of lung cancer. He had never given any signs of being other than an enthusiastic teacher who never displayed much of the warmer side of his nature. All his talk was of ideas and concepts; he was a man's man and never showed any sign of weakness. Yet, at the end, when he could no

.... at the beginning, we are simple enough to ad-

mit that we need the touch of someone who cares.

At that time I didn't know about healing prayer, and only saw the human dimension of his loneliness and his reaching out his hand for help. But since then I have come to realize the wisdom of the gospel writers, encouraging us to lay our hands upon the sick, for I now realize that the love of God flows through our hands to radiate the sick area with God's healing power, to wither up the sickness and to enliven all the healthy cells to fight the body's enemies!

Last, there does come a time for every-one to die, and one of the simplest, most beautiful things you can do for a friend who is dying is simply be there, holding his hand, caring for him until he moves from this life to the next. Often the question comes, "Should I pray for the healing of an elderly person who seems to be dying?" If you ask God in prayer whether you should pray for healing or not and are still not sure, I would recommend doing what a sister who is a nurse has discovered is most natural in the situation: She simply prays that Jesus pour his *life* into the person. Then Jesus can make the decision whether that life is entrance into the new life which is heaven, or whether that life heals the sick person's body and restores it to physical health. In any case, you can simply sit by the sick person's bedside, saying a prayer here or there, but mostly just holding the person's hand, picturing the life of Jesus in you flowing into your sick friend, healing and comforting.

I remember vividly, when my father and my mother died, just four months apart, what a strength it was to have several Christian friends who took turns with me over the last few nights. I would not have had the strength to do it alone, but together we could be there at that transition from life to that new life which we call death. From time to time we would say a prayer, or read a sentence or two

Only the love that brings and sustains life,
often in silence.

Ten

Inner Healing

Of all the healings most of us need, the deepest, the one we need most, is usually spiritual or emotional. So often when I have given weekend retreats, the group was loudly praising God and seemed so happy on Friday evening. Then afterward our team was available to pray with individuals for a blessing in any area they wanted. We didn't offer to pray for healing. We wanted to begin in a positive way, praying for a blessing and leaving the heavier healings for the next day. But, over and over, as people came forward for a blessing, the happy smile would disappear and they would utter a cry from the heart for inner healing: "Please pray for me. I've been thinking of suicide since my husband left me"; "Please pray because I'm in great confusion. I'm a homosexual and every so often I start cruising the streets looking for someone, and I can't seem to help it"; "I'm just plain anxious and fearful. I don't know what's wrong, but I don't like being with people."

Beneath that celebration a few minutes before, most of the group were suffering in very deep ways. Some of that suffering is just part of the cross and comes with any normal human situation, the "vale of tears" that is life. Some of the suffering calls for repentance and a change in the person's way of life. But a large part of the suffering results from the emotional wounds of the past which Jesus came to heal so that we might become a "new creation" (2 Cor 5:17).

To me, the greatest discovery in the healing ministry has been that Jesus *commonly* heals these deep wounds.

> The spirit of the Lord Yahweh has been
> given to me,

for Yahweh has anointed me.
He has sent me to bring good news to the poor...
to bind up hearts that are broken (Is 61:1).

So far as I know, it was Agnes Sanford, now
in her eighties, who was the first to discover
in a practical way how Jesus might actually
heal these wounds, for he walked back with
her into her past and healed her of the mental
depression which, like the years of the locust,
had kept her bound for seven years.

What we have discovered for ourselves
(it is already there in Scripture) is that every
part of Jesus, every aspect of his own emotional and mental makeup died with him
upon the cross for our redemption. He was a
human being like us in everything except sin.

> For it is not as if we had a high priest who
> was incapable of feeling our weaknesses with
> us; but we have one who was tempted in
> every way that we are, though he is without
> sin. Let us be confident, then, in ap-
> proaching the throne of grace, that we shall
> have mercy from him and find grace when
> we are in need of help (Hb 4:15-16).

When Jesus cried out "I thirst" something in
him was dying that the alcoholic might not
thirst again. When he cried on the cross, "My
God, why have you deserted me?" he suffered the felt loss of his Father that we might
know the Father's presence: "We shall come
to him and make our home with him" (Jn
14:23).

For all the interior weaknesses that we
have, Jesus promises us a share of his own
life and personality. We are meant to share in
his love for his Father and his people; we are
meant to share in his joy and in his peace.
We are not just to try to be peaceful, with him
as model, but we are also to ask for his peace
as a gift, beyond anything we can achieve by
all our discipline and effort: "Peace I bequeath
to you, my own peace I give you, a peace
the world cannot give, this is my gift to you"
(Jn 14:27). This is not to say we don't need
to try to do as much as we can to love, to be
at peace, to be joyful, to be patient, but
beyond a point we are bound to fail unless we
ask for them as gifts, for they are fruits of the
Holy Spirit.

Because of our fallen, wounded condition as human beings, we all find ourselves in the sad situation described by St. Paul, "I can not understand my own behaviour. I fail to carry out the things I want to do, and I find myself doing the very things I hate" (Rom 7:15). The good news is that all this compulsive action can be healed. The completion of healing usually takes time, but often there are quantum leaps of healing as we pray.

The study of psychology is helpful in pointing out the roots of our sickness and how the evil in people and in the world twists our personalities. But while psychology is strong on the human analysis of our problems, it is not so strong on cure. With the help of Jesus, however, we can get at the childhood wounds that hinder our growth and compel us to act in ways that we know are wrong but can't seem to help. I find that almost always when we have time to pray with a person over a course of time, wonderful changes begin to take place.

Just take the following statement from a woman we prayed with last month:

It seems to me that when darkness reigns within, you do not realize what it's like to be free. Well, I feel great. All my life a mocking ring sounded whenever I tried to love the Lord or carry out my tasks in life. The last time I heard it was just before the spirit of rejection was cast out.[1] The result—I feel good about my decisions and myself. The other day an angry woman came at me and, for the first time, her anger never touched me. Wow! It's like being in a dream and hoping that the peace I experience is for real . . . and forever.

Socializing has always been an agony for me. But now I feel good about parties and being with people. (I used to make up any excuse in any situation to get away from people.)

One of the greatest changes in me is a new vitality. I do not feel tired all the time. My whole life has been a war against fatigue . . . finding fast and easy ways to do my work so that when weariness came, I would be free to rest (sometimes 12 hours a day). Oh, do I feel good!

1. Along with the inner healing there was also some deliverance from evil spirits.

For myself, I have healed inner healing mostly in the area of fear of people — a common affliction in our society. I grew up in an atmosphere where I wanted to compete in studies, in popularity and in sports. Like most people I often failed. As a 135-pound, 6-foot 3-inch graduate of high school I was gawky and awkward and carried a deep inner shyness and embarrassment for years afterwards, even after I gained a little more weight. It was only through prayer that I was released so I could more or less forget myself and go about my work without being so self-conscious. As I did, most people carry around deep-seated fears or bitterness that prevents them from having the freedom that belongs to the children of God.

How can we go about praying for that inner freedom we so much desire and need?

Well, there are some simple ways that can help most of us, although the more difficult cases may need the help of someone specially gifted in prayer, or a professional counselor, or, ideally, someone who combines both a special gift in prayer and professional training.

The simplest, most basic way of receiving inner healing is to ask a friend who is close to the Lord to help you. (Ideally, this would be your husband or your wife, or perhaps your mother or your father, or a member of your community.) Then set aside a time, an hour or so, when you will not be rushed.

Next, share whatever area of your life needs to be healed: when the problem started (if you know); the key incidents in your life that contributed to it; and how other people may have contributed to the problem or even caused it. (For instance, we are discovering that an extraordinary number of women were molested as young girls, sometimes by fathers or brothers, and this leaves deep scars that later may affect their relationships with their husbands.) Share with your prayer partner, as best you can, that area of your life, together with the roots of the problem. These roots often go very far back into childhood or, occasionally, even before birth.[2] Most of these

2. In the actual praying, several people I know suddenly

wounds go back to specific incidents or to relationships that went wrong. Relationships with fathers and mothers and embarrassing in events in school seem especially common sources of these wounds.

For most of us it is very difficult to share in depth about ourselves and our weaknesses. Many people cry when they vividly remember the painful days of the past. But it is healing even to be able to bring yourself to the point of sharing these experiences in depth with one or two other persons. It is a great sign of trust to be able to tell another person the truth about your life. For me, to talk is a source of strength. And for you to listen heals me on the human level. We condemn ourselves so deeply that we are helped by having someone listen who does not condemn us, but simply listens.

Jesus was left alone with the woman, who

---

found themselves re-experiencing things most of us cannot consciously remember—impressions going back to the time they were carried in their mother's womb. Experiences like these have helped me realize, even more deeply than before, the tragedy of abortion.

remained standing there. He looked up and said, "Woman, where are they? Has no one condemned you?" "No one, sir" she replied. "Neither do I condemn you," said Jesus, "go away, and don't sin any more" (Jn 8: 9-11).

Because it is so painful to share these memories and because it takes time to even try, many married people have never shared themselves at this deepest level. As a result they don't really understand each other. When one of those raw nerves that were exposed in early childhood is touched, the explosion of pain or anger that results cannot be understood without understanding the source. If those of you who are married would only set aside time to be with each other and to share your lives and to pray together, it would help immeasurably in knowing each other and in healing each other so those flawed relationships of the past could not harm your present life together.

Ideally, your sharing would be with a person with whom you can be totally honest, someone who would understand if you broke down and cried and who would know that

...crying is healthy, who would also know that you might need to be held if you cried. Clearly, though, there could be difficulties if an unmarried man and woman were praying alone in this situation, so, for a single person it is often best to go to an understanding married couple for prayer. (I have seen a great deal of healing go on when individuals were held while they cried, so it is good to have a situation where this can happen without the danger of its being misunderstood or abused in a sexual way.)

After you have shared as best and as deeply as you can about that area of your life that still has the power to affect you harmfully, then it is time for praying. This prayer relies on two things:

1) that Jesus was a human being like you, and that his humanity suffered in that very area where you need healing so that you might be healed;

2) that Jesus can walk back into the past and change its effects upon your present life in a way that neither you nor any psychiatrist can.

So, your friend can pray for you—or you can pray for your friend—asking Jesus to walk back and to take the poison out of your past. (It is very much like the prayer we described in the chapter on forgiveness.) A simple way is to ask the person you are praying for to imagine the harmful incident, and then to imagine Jesus coming into the picture, doing each of the things that would have healed the situation at that time.

The person doing the praying can either ask Jesus to come into the picture and then *be silent while Jesus takes over and does those things that are necessary* (he really seems to do this in a certain number of cases—and these are the best, for healing always takes place). Or, the person praying can be sensitive to the inspiration of the Holy Spirit, and *pray out loud* and *describe* the various things that Jesus would do if he had been present.

The following examples will give you an idea of some of the ways Jesus has healed.

Once a woman prayed for her own healing because she had experienced a very unhappy childhood dominated by a cold and critical mother who made life miserable for her at home. In the prayer Jesus appeared and took the little girl into the laundry room where she had received many scoldings, and simply talked and sang with her and helped her fold the wash. He totally transformed that miserable memory of her home by spending a long time helping her to enjoy her work—something she had not been able to do (not simply the laundry, but all her work).

Another time I was praying with a man who felt distance from God as the result of a harsh religious education. While we prayed, Jesus appeared to him as he remembered seeing him in a picture on the wall of his childhood bedroom—seated and surrounded by little children, some on his lap, some on the ground. In the beginning of this vision he, as a boy, was seated on the ground, looking away from Jesus, for this was how he felt—alone and rejected. Then Jesus picked him up and set him on his lap, turning him around in the process. As he faced him, Jesus smiled and all feelings of rejection and distance from God dissolved.

I give you these two very simple examples because they show what I have observed about the way Jesus works: He often heals the *undramatic* hurts so many people have experienced, such as painful loneliness, as well as healing the dramatic calamities that usually dominate the testimonies at banquets. When he heals he often uses very simple, everyday ways of being present such as setting a child on his lap or helping a person work at a humdrum task.

Praying for inner healing, then, can be very simple. Just sit down next to the other person and put your hand on his shoulder or in his hand. Then ask Jesus to go back and heal each wounded relationship, each painful incident. Pray either in silence, letting Jesus do it all or, with God's inspiration, pray out loud what you imagine Jesus would do to make the person whole.

As you gain experience, you may also wish to ask God the *Father* to walk back and

Help if the person you are praying for had a broken relationship with his or her father. For Catholics, especially, we find that Jesus often sends his mother Mary who, in her humanity, can make up for whatever was missing in the person's relationship with the mother.

It is very hard to tell you how to do this, because each person you pray with is so different. It is a mistake to imply that any formula prayer can cover the multitude of ways in which God's people have been wounded and the widely different ways that God himself goes about healing them. To explain how in this chapter would be difficult, if not impossible. But if you realize that the idea of inner healing is very simple, if you realize that inner healing almost always takes place (more than physical healing), you should be encouraged to pray for the people closest to you. Just listen to your friend's problem and, without pretending to analyze or judge or figure it out, begin to pray in simple ways, following the lead of the Spirit. You may find yourself picturing Jesus helping in all kinds of ways that you know you would never have

thought of on your own. Most of the ways
Jesus heals are very simple: He forgives people, he looks them in the eye, and the way
he looks at them heals the ancient rejection;
he holds them in his arms like a brother and
the loneliness melts away.

One way he heals is remarkably simple:
Many parents know that they have harmed
their children's spiritual or emotional growth
because of something they once did or said.
Yet, the parents may not be able to voice the
problem to the child without making it worse.
If they pray in tongues, though, the mother
and father can simply put their hands upon
the child while the child is asleep, then pray
in tongues and ask God to use the prayer to
bring inner healing. Several parents I know
have tried this very simple method and found
dramatic changes in the child's attitude and
actions the very next day!

In fact, the whole idea of praying for inner healing is so simple that we may reject it:
"Such a complicated, deep-rooted problem
can't be changed by such a simple prayer!"

recesses of the heart. He alone can bring you the peace that the world cannot give.

Epilogue

I hope by now you are encouraged to put into practice some of these very simple sugges-
tions; they can change your life. I trust also
that you will see Jesus do wonderful things in
and through you. It is all so remarkably simple that it's hard to understand why more
Christians have not been doing it; basically, all
it involves is
  —having compassion and love for people,
  —believing that Jesus has far more concern
    than you do (as well as the power to do
    something about it),
  —speaking to Jesus and asking him to heal,
  —and resting your hands upon the sick.

You have nothing to lose (other than pride) by trying, and a whole new world will open up for you in which you will see God's compassion at work.

My prayer for you is this:

Lord Jesus, give faith and confidence to the ones who read these words, so that they will want to reach out their hands to their friends and pray that pain will disappear and sickness will be healed. Give them wisdom to know how best to pray; fill their prayers with the faith that heals and their hands with the power that gives life and comfort. As they launch out and begin to pray with their families and friends, let them know you more deeply than ever before. Let them experience the wonder and surprises of the friend you are: Jesus Christ, our Lord, our healer and our friend.

Amen

Billy Graham	**Jennifer Rees Larcombe**
Michael Green	**Cliff Richard**
Michele Guinness	**John Stott**
Joyce Huggett	**Joni Eareckson Tada**
Francis MacNutt	**Colin Urquhart**
Catherine Marshall	**David Watson**
Jim Packer	**David Wilkerson**
Adrian Plass	**John Wimber**

The wide range of books on the Hodder Christian
Paperback list include **biography, personal testimony,
devotional books, evangelistic books, Christian teaching,
fiction, drama, poetry, books that give help for times of
need** – and many others.

Ask at your nearest Christian bookshop or at your church
bookstall for the latest titles.

SOME BESTSELLERS IN HODDER CHRISTIAN PAPERBACKS

THE HIDING PLACE by Corrie ten Boom

The triumphant story of Corrie ten Boom, heroine of the anti-Nazi underground.

"A brave and heartening story."

Baptist Times

GOD'S SMUGGLER by Brother Andrew

An international bestseller. God's Smuggler carries contraband Bibles past armed border guards to bring the love of Christ to the people behind the Iron Curtain.

"A book you will not want to miss."

Catherine Marshall

DISCIPLESHIP by David Watson

". . . breath-taking, block-busting, Bible-based simplicity on every page."

Jim Packer

LISTENING TO GOD by Joyce Huggett

A profound spiritual testimony, and practical help for discovering a new dimension of prayer.

"This is counselling at its best."

Leadership Today

CELEBRATION OF DISCIPLINE by Richard Foster

A classic on the spiritual Disciplines.

RUN BABY RUN by Nicky Cruz with Jamie Buckingham

A tough New York gang leader discovers Christ.

"It is a thrilling story. My hope is that it shall have a wide reading."

Billy Graham

CHASING THE DRAGON by Jackie Pullinger with Andrew Quicke

Life-changing miracles in Hong Kong's Walled City.

"A book to stop you in your tracks."

Liverpool Daily Post

BORN AGAIN by Charles Colson

Disgraced by Watergate, Charles Colson finds a new life.

"An action packed story of real life drama and a revelation of modern history as well as a moving personal account."

Elim Evangel

KNOWING GOD by J I Packer

The biblical portrait that has become a classic.

"(The author) illumines every doctrine he touches and commends it with courage, logic, lucidity and warmth . . . the truth he handles fires the heart. At least it fired mine, and compelled me to turn aside to worship and pray."

John Stott

THE HAPPIEST PEOPLE ON EARTH by Demos Shakarian with John and Elizabeth Sherrill

The extraordinary beginnings of the Full Gospel Business Men's Fellowship.